Manolo Ameixeiras

Twenty-Nine unattainable poems

Manolo Ameixeiras

Twenty-Nine unattainable poems

JustFiction Edition

Imprint

Cover image: www.ingimage.com

Publisher:
JustFiction! Edition
is a trademark of
Dodo Books Indian Ocean Ltd., member of the OmniScriptum S.R.L Publishing group
str. A.Russo 15, of. 61, Chisinau-2068, Republic of Moldova Europe
Printed at: see last page
ISBN: 978-620-3-57571-2

TWENTY-NINE
UNATTAINABLE POEMS
O Poeta
MANOLO
AMEIXEIRAS

I

Your eyes

Undefined reflection,
ephemeral precision of...
Loneliness of need,
touch of
indifference.
Difference of passion
passion of being
soul being
soul of two.
Your eyes
reflection of...
of both of us.

II

Come back

Return to walk
in starry hours
starry hours of the night
the demagogic fissures
of the palpitation.
Return to be
in electric of thought,
the dramaturgical fissures
of the palpitation.
The roots return
in autumn?
No!.

Fermented opening
of latex?.

The ghosts return

to be
in daylight hours
of the ethyl palpitate.
Will come back?
Something!
 will return

Won't come back.

III

I will pray 1/3

To seek ½

To take you at ¼

IV

The fool in love

So, so, so much.
So, so, so, so in love.
In love like a fool
what a foolish
of a fool.
How young, so much
how it's so silly
as is so much love
What a fool's love
What a fool of a love.
He gets drunk
and dies
what a fool
so much formaldehyde

made a fool.
He opened the bottle:
and said

Babes!...

I just got out.
Who was the fool
and so much, and so much
so much, so much love
But it's love

Of a fool.

V

Odd

Are days
the dim street lights
strolled indifferent
under the equalized shadow
of little Vip locals.

The days
the blue sky of Canary islands
was turning dark
unmistakable symptom
of lonely winter
that was approaching.

Those days

could be said
that lies separated them
were the fruit of a sincerity
so confused
as thinking the future.
Would be say...
the lies,
or the truths;
what are?

Those days
someone swore
sitting on a sofa
Never again!...
But then... he went out...
the balcony!
He drew a smile face.
Say himself :
What the fuck!
He looked the bar.

Days...

a plane left.

VI

OR NOT

Are.
The days
so full
empty.
Days narrow
so juicy
idyllic.
Days
When love you
without being
no time.
Must be days,
after the nights,
filled
so emptys.

Are days
 I return ...
 to need you.

VII

TURURU

Guava tomb elea
fastness bravo drawing
bodys cojunudos fucking,
interruptus motocultor noise.

Tremendous anger unleashed!
dust, sheets, floor
body, feet, cold, sweat...

Words
blah, blah, blah!

Female reaction
desire

go on...
Shut up!
Go back to bed
smile, ...
Let's get down to business
ah,
ah,
oh...!
JO!
Already?....

Explain
noise not possible
were missing!

Female
clothes, sofa...
escape...
Go hell!

Guava tomb elea
nefarious bravo drawing

bodys cojunudos fucking,
interruptus noise motocultor .

Brrrruuuumh brrrruuuumh
brrrruuuumh brrrruuuumh!

IX

LIVE IN?

Live on?
Santiago

Where is your room?
In home. Yes!

Santiago!
In your bed, not?

Santiago, yes,yes!.

Have gray...
Santiago.

Live on!

Have gray to much!
Santiago.

Jewel mine!...
Montillón
Montillón.
I am from Montillón!
live!.
What do you think about
the inmortally of the crab?
Sorry i never speak about
animals!.
Don´t touch
the eggs from Montillón.
NON : NON!.

X

WINS

Desire to...

fucking desire?

No fucking desire

want to whore?

no fucking desire whores?

without wins!

want to desire!

whithout whores?

wins?

Whithout whores?

XI

Know randomness
is disguised
on odd days.

Know different
does not exists
implores.

Know things
are disguise as goodness
at envy
is being destroyed.

We know!.

but slowly.

You and I ...
are one.

Know
I love you
We know ...
it was necessary!.

Already know more?...

already...

It's time!.

XII

MY TRUTH...LOVE

A quake on your lips,
open!
A look!

A fallen god
drag is!
In the miseries
of your mind.

Why your lips...
do not close...

Why does time stop?
When I look at ?
Why?... why?...

Why is ?

I got scared!
I run away?

Why, run away?
Why I can't run away?

I didn't fall in love, never?
I never fell in love!
Why?

Return!, why?.

Why?
Why?

XIII

YES?....

All is easier!
It is?
Says, don't ?

All is easier?

I complicate it!

Is easier?
Why is it easier?

The same demon,
has expelled me from hell!

"Get out of here!"
"Only come here to warm up,

make a mess"!

All is easier!
Why do I mess it up?.

I just wanted to know...

Yes!

XIII

Lost you!

Formulus eternus,
fuck people .
Infinite fight
sale excluded.

Formulas abound...
female replete,
secrets segregate.

Laborer land remenber
formulas female language, at
ejem...!

Intense boiling, lost struggle;
memories, codes, lies.
Epic whispers break...

mythical horses;
without ears, on the bolk.

Economic liberalisms
sexus, masturbation est!.
benefits, accommodations,
residences, financial concessions.

Bedding arches,
variable height,
adjustable position,
removable illusion.

Laborer think...
Farm is not big enough!

XIV

A THOUSAND MEMORIES

I had to travel
Yes!
I know... no one understands.
Had to erase
Yes!
I know... no one understands.

My ghosts
had to...
I know... nobody understands.
An elliptical meandering
took me...
to the philosopher's cave!

In damnation
perennial inconsistency
of putrefied meat...
blossomed.
I had to travel!
Yes!
I had to...
die!

Gosh, what blow!.

I had to come back!

But I brought
ghosts.

Honey...
have pets!.

Gosh, what blow!.

Who are you?

What have you done to me?

I had to come back!
Is not true!
It does not happen !

Erased memories
speaking...
speaking.

But...
I have...
thousand memories.

What...

Record by your side.

XV

DILEMMA

Static dilemma
Analytical difference
Syntactic influences
Illusions of return.
          Forms
                    Ideas
                                        Dilemmas
Dark phases
Electric, switched.

Distant different
Alluvions in meanders
Euphoric dilemmas; hot
Forms. there?
                    Here?.

Fashionable snatches
Photos
Phytos
Filomos
Fofo
Dilemmas of progress!

Ephemeral essences!

XVI

SWALLOS

Birds
whit so much feather.
black or white?
White or black!.

Arrive in spring
Rest and go on

In the end
A day of feathers
a day of feathers!
Empty
At hand are made to fly
will not return...
vultures?
At random feather

of goodbye,
Derisory form
of nothing
nothing of nothing!
All in nothing
At melt
nothing...
Swallows are flying
and way to fly!

Well bye!

XVII

Brute things... to things beautiful

I think... I understand
God, is always waiting...
every step of the way
Is a learning.
start to forget
So many things...
have left
traces in soul.
But
slowly... slowly
I have to learn
to manage...
Here I go again
I think I understand...

Will see!
Nadia
People don't change
I seen it.
One who was an asshole;
he gives up drugs...
and he is an asshole.
don't change, it's impossible.
But well;
an act of faith!
It's impossible!

Change!
but the world does not change...
has followed its course;
and it is the same.
What happens?
As it is impossible;
I cool.

It turns out;
Maybe,
You no longer laugh at your friends;
You don't feel like playing the role attribute to you...
and
of course!
it is impossible!
But nothing is impossible!
So I even like it.
artist, the other one, the one on the motorcycle....
You?
Facebook?
I like it... but.
made things;
and an idiot likes it.
Are you an idiot?
No... I don't know.
You like it?;
fuck you,

and are also an idiot.
You don't like it, fine...
I respect you just as much or more.
Maybe..;
You don't need to like
Let's see;
Are not stupid,
Don't you know right or wrong?
Okay... you think!
I change name?
You do!

Open another day.
Look at pet!
What do I care about your mascot?.
Likes sixty!

A bird!

Don't miss it! In a cage!

Do I like it?
No fucking way!
You think !
What am I doing here?
All people masturbating each other!
Go out!
Fuck no!
He don´t let you.
Why are you leaving?
the reason?
In the end you get it...
You deleted!
you do.
Act of faith!
Change recklessness.
Are on your own!
You see!
But no, don't change!
It is impossible.
But loneliness and you, you

already know each other... you are
old friends.
It's impossible!
It's cool. You go ahead.

But who wants to be alone?
Think about her;
exists?.
You think?...

Ecco
Ricominciare.

XVIII

YOU ARE BLUE

Pop
Pop that?
Pop that no?

The musician slips
over the polluted air
his warm hands.

Some people
wait for the bus.

The workers
they drag in heavy days
their unwillingness.

It would be
Pop
Pop that!
Pop that not?

She plays with her hair
he stares at her fixedly.

The piano
sounds to empty bottles.

They talk...

Pop
Pop that
Pop that not!

Pedestrians look like
pissed off ants.
The mutilated snake
is a streetcar.

Angry words
come out of the radio.

That would be
Pop?

Pop that!

Pop that not?

XIX

THE FAILIURE

In the chronicles
from nowhere!

Figures, or not!

Inconsistent shadows
Of a goodbye.
You've already done it!
What's left for you?

Failure!

But, if you haven't tried?

On the sidewalk.
Waiting for your eyes
Painted on
The window
That doesn't stop
The train of memory
has forgotten...
The tavern of the sky
Where I drank
Yours
Ours
The eyes
Screens
Maybe
It's just things
Enough!
Where the struggle of space
Never ended
To be one
Shoes, shoes
Travelers, travelers

Our words
Distant, Close...
We two of the same substance
Only iron
Future rust
Then
Nothing
The End
I remain alone

I walk, walk , walk.

On the sidewalk.

XX

They are fossil@.es

SOSpirables to the near

SOSpirables at close range

They are elliptical

S.O.S

XXI

GOOGBYE

That life is this!
Let the sun rise!
JE, JE!
That a drop of water, can be....

But brother, life is struggle.
Fight and struggle.

Don't leave every sunset;
look the little beautiful things;
fill your eyes with light;
understand that tomorrow does
not exist.

But brother!
That life is this!

The sun sets!
Laughing can be vital.

Have a good fight. Have a good journey. Fight and struggle.

THIS IS WHAT LIFE IS ALL ABOUT!

XXII

ABOUT THAT?

We burst with bad luck
In the empty world
Without room For another.

--He don't understand. I'm pregnant

--You don't understand. It seems like...

Fruit of love. There is nothing. Nothing

We have killed,
The naked aberration of

speaking...
In the hidden cowardice of living.

All have died. In the race of life.

Maybe!

Are we all a little sleepy?

XXIII

LIFE

A sweet word.

A beloved heart.

A close hand...
Or a lovable smile.
These are the things of life.

I want to be a seagull.
I want to laugh and live.
I want to understand! Why?
With so many questions.
It's life in things!

Saying the right things.

Making things be good.

Understanding that everything is a result of love.

IS THE JOY OF LIFE.

XXIV

ON SIDEWALK

Maybe things are bad.
However, I don't come to
understand; why...
I don't know the substance
wrapped.
Maybe, the same thing is
beautiful.

I was waiting for your eyes.

I can't understand.
I don't want understand.
I don't want come any
conclusion.

I am distracted ; upset in my
thoughts.
There is nothing ... nothing.

A hole in space, cracking.
A little air! Polluted. Is the cage...
Of my thoughts
Is the haste they bring, the
travelers.
A hole in space, cracking.

Maybe; a little worry.
Maybe!
Little non-concern, little non-
quiet. Maybe even...

These shoes.
It's second time, that passed!
Yes.
With same pants. I staying here
too long.

Maybe things
Are

Just things
A train arrives... I look it

I'm sitting in illusory chair.
Between two marble pillars; facing the platform.
With my head down. I see no one. I look only the shoes.

They are your eyes; painted on...
That window, that doesn't stop.
It's the train of memory; that has forgotten
many lies.
Shoes! Dirty shoes, clean shoes...
Worn out, smooth .
Sports shoes, leather shoes.
Shoes and more shoes; just shoes slipping over sidewalk.

Slowly. With stress. Fast; or just...
desperate.
Unhurriedly. With weariness

Travelers go out... Cigarettes.
Friends.

Travelers drag their heavy luggage.

I almost thought?...

LOOK AT ME BICHT

I believed in you!

XXV

THE SOUND OF THINKING

I don't want think
why...

Because
the uncertainty ladies
or, perhaps
that's life.

Because
the lies are gone
or maybe
a new love.

Because

wherever I go
they;
cannot follow me...
my ghosts!

Because
the semantics of my brain
deconstructed in delirium
has decided to
work and work.

Because
the truth!.
already

I DON'T THINK!

GREAT DISCOVERY, OR NOT?

XXVI

YES CLEAR

With certain power jumps.
An isolated system
Subatomic reality works,
or not.
And I
I look myself!
And don't see
yes, of course.
A particle can be
how two particles so far apart
in these properties
you see, you!
I run and run
with my hands

the tights of your stockings...
And, in the heat
Yes!
To design capable technologies
to understand how microscopic
microscopic parts work
and when it circulates it is "on".

Ephemeral tongues
pierce my eardrums
and you?
You burn memories
of low estimation...
down there in the depths
in the heat!
Say it.
You survive and come out reborn.

XXVII

WHAT IS YOUR STORY

A phone number
the mortgage
a white lie.
Twice, or three times a week
life.
So what?
That painter of bad life,
and you idiot
who are you for?.
Some algorithm
that speaks...
aphorisms.
Maybe...

an idea, that's true...
if you can.
I don't know.
A kite
that you built a child,
a love, that wasn't.

A book
cursed
a recurring nightmare?
Perhaps...
a success, deserved,
or not?
NO...
MY STORY... IS NOT

XXVIII

ERRORS

A diagnosed delusion,
a metaphysical farce
a return the past.

Many things that are not so
you were right.
Not like that!
But you forgot to tell me how.
Well I made it up...
maybe I installed
the wrong drivers.
Y
somewhere.
When the words speak

about you,
I will always say that didn't get
the tattoo.
Culture asserts itself as a
privileged instrument;

the truth is,
the sanity
is so much hypocrisy.

Culture or agriculture?
That is the question.

We already knew . Didn't we?

XXIX

WITH THE DAYS AHEAD

With the days ahead
the past dissipates
becomes alien, distant
and the future a trail happiness.

With the days ahead
your tired eyes will return
in search of refuge
and when you find
you will live intensely...
 be worth all tears
past tears.

With the days ahead
you'll know
nothing bad matters anymore,
you'll feel peace and rest.

With the days ahead.
I want to pass on
you some of my strength,
 my love...
 keep you on your way.

With the days ahead
you will hear the language
the plants
you will listen
the free birds like you
you will know how
drink the pure water
you will enjoy yourself
like never before.

With the days ahead
those swallows
will return
our balcony will hang their nests
you will whisper
the wind the word freedom
and you will live it.

With the days ahead
nothing is unfair
nothing is ethereal
everything is you...
old and young friend
full of freedom in trial of choice.

With the days ahead
I chose your smile
to deposit it all my being
and I have seen
it again in your eyes
eternal mirrors of a free world.

With the days ahead
love
will take possession
your body
to be free.

MANOLO

AMEIXEIRAS

va por ti
MR PAINT
suso muras
que estas en los
cielos

Printed by Books on Demand GmbH, Norderstedt / Germany